Irresistibly GlutenFree
Simple Family Favorite Recipes

Irresistibly GlutenFree
Simple Family Favorite Recipes

by Christina Davis

Library of Congress Control Number: 2010929688

Be sure to consult with a doctor before changing your diet.
The author takes no responsibility for the health of users
of *Irresistibly Gluten Free: Simple Family Favorite Recipes*.
It is the user's responsibility to check labels of product
ingredients to ensure they are gluten free.

First printing 2010
10 9 8 7 6 5 4 3 2 1
Printed in the United States.

Recipe photographs
by Shawn Robins Photography
www.shawnrobins.com

Table of Contents

Dedicated to...

My talented and supportive husband Rob. You rock!

And my six not-so-small-anymore bundles of inspiration:
Coby, Bridger, Keaton, McCall, Emerald, and Barek.

Special thanks to...

My father, Arnold, for his celiac genes.

Paul Rawlins and Jennifer Utley for their editorial expertise and general book know-how. Melanie Gunnell for her cooking genius and great advice.

Shawn and Jen Robins for their time and care in photographing (and later eating) the food, and to Mataio and Jessica Gillis at Ciao Thyme (www.CiaoThyme.com) for the use of their beautiful catering kitchen in Bellingham, Washington.

My local Gluten Intolerance Group in Logan, especially Annette Bryner and Georgia Rawlings.

And all the friends who tested my recipes and encouraged me along the way.

Introduction

Irresistibly Gluten Free is a cookbook created to make food enjoyable again for anyone restricted to a gluten-free diet. As the mother of 6 children I have had plenty of experience with picky eaters, three of whom are on a gluten-free diet. I know how discouraging it can be to spend a lot of time and money on food that no one will eat. I hope these recipes will be as helpful to you as they have been to me.

Cooking gluten free can be a bumpy road. After fifteen years of trial and error, I have come up with some solutions that pave the way to stress-free cooking for the celiac, or anyone on a gluten-free diet.

These recipes are not only gluten free, but they are simple to make, affordable, and taste so much like their wheat equivalent you will be excited to eat again! All the ingredients can be found in most grocery stores. And most of the recipes can be made milk- (casein-) free as well.

Cooking for kids is hard enough without restrictions, but take away their white bread, corn dogs, and chicken nuggets and you find yourself in a nightmare. This cookbook is specifically designed to help you feed your child who has had all their favorites taken away. And the good news is, the food tastes so good your whole family will be able to enjoy it, and you won't spend all your time making two different versions of every meal.

One of the unavoidable bumps in the gluten-free cooking road is the fact that you can't take the short cuts. Fast food is difficult, frozen or prepackaged meals are generally not an option. You get to do all the cooking from now on. But I have found ways to make cooking easier and less time consuming. In this book I will share tips that save time and offer shortcuts that you can take to make your job easier.

You will feel a satisfaction worth all your effort when you hear your kids say "Wow, this is great! Will you make it again?" And knowing that they are healthier by sticking to their gluten-free diet will give you peace of mind. The recipes in this book are not super nutritious; it is not a health food cookbook. Most gluten-free foods have little protein or little nutritional value. So I suggest you include fresh fruits and vegetables in every meal. By eating this way your gluten-free kids are more healthy and still able to enjoy their favorite foods.

So, eat up kids! These recipes have been kid tested and kid approved. And everyone knows, when the kids are happy, Mom is happy too!

Cooking Tips

There are a few things you have to do differently when cooking gluten free. If you follow these rules you will have more success cooking from this book.

Read It Before You Eat It

The most important rule to remember when cooking gluten free is to read every label to ensure you are not adding any gluten to your food. Gluten can be found in some of the most unsuspected places. And often the products you have relied on for years suddenly show up containing gluten. (I found gluten in some butterscotch chips while making cookies the other day!) If you are new to the gluten-free diet and have trouble remembering what to look for on food labels I recommend you keep a copy of all glutenous key words (usually the doctor who diagnosed you has already given you this information, or you can find it from a credible website) and keep a copy in your purse or wallet so you can refer to it while shopping.

Mixing Correctly

It is important to always put the dry ingredients in the mixer first, and then pour in the wet while the mixer is running. Because there is cornstarch in the UNflour, it won't mix well and can become lumpy if you don't follow this method. I like to put all the dry ingredients in the bowl of my mixer and all the wet ingredients in a large, glass measuring cup. This not only makes it less messy to measure out the wet ingredients, but it makes it easier to pour in the wet while the mixer is running.

Adjust for Altitude

Gluten-free cooking can be touchy. The amounts and temperatures I have listed in the recipes work great for me here in a dry, high altitude. If you live at a lower, more humid altitude you may find it necessary to adjust the amount of liquid you need in your recipes or the temperature you cook them at. I have made many of these recipes while visiting near the West Coast and didn't find it too difficult. Just add all but the last ½ cup or so of wet ingredients and watch your batters or doughs. Add the remaining liquid, or extra liquid, as needed. You will get used to how it should look after just a couple tries. But don't be hard on yourself it things go wrong once in a while. It happens to everyone, and I tell you, I can never explain how or why it does that.

Xanthan Gum

The one ingredient you can't do without is the xanthan gum. It is the binder that holds the flour together. If you prefer guar gum you can substitute it, but you will need to adjust the amount. To substitute guar gum for xanthan gum use 1 teaspoon of guar gum for every ¾ teaspoons xanthan gum. I find xanthan gum works better for my recipes, and I don't tolerate the natural laxative effect of guar gum well, so I have used xanthan in all my recipes.

Flour Substitutions

If you can't eat cornstarch or tapioca flour you can try substituting potato starch. You will have to experiment with the amount, but it should work pretty well. Also, you can substitute other gluten-free flours for the rice flour such as sorghum, quinoa, or garfava bean flour. Again, you will have to experiment, and the taste will be affected quite a lot.

Nutrition

Most gluten-free cookbooks I have used in the past try to add nutrition to the gluten-free products by using bean flours or odd ingredients (like egg replacer) that do not help the taste of the food. This only discouraged my children from eating at all. My recipes do not use "health food store" ingredients; they are designed to be simple and taste like real food

so kids will eat them. There are lots of good, whole foods they can eat, like fresh fruits and vegetables. So get the nutrition from those foods and allow the gluten-free products to taste good. I do like to use almond meal in place of instant dry milk in my breads because it improves the nutritional value, but it also keeps the bread moist longer and improves the taste. It can be hard to find almond meal, so I often make my own by grinding whole almonds in my food processor.

Milk and Sugar Substitutes

I have heard many celiacs say that milk and/or sugar is hard for them to digest. We have found this to be true at our house. I also know many children are on the GFCF Diet (gluten-free, casein-free diet).

I have used organic evaporated cane juice sugar in all of these recipes and found them to work just as well and taste great too.

Many of the recipes call for milk, but I have added "or milk substitute" to all of the recipes that I have successfully been able to use rice milk or soy milk in.

There are a few recipes that can not be made milk free. The Cream Soup Mix is one, but you can use the seasonings from the

Cream Soup Mix and add them to your milk substitute with the cornstarch to make a soup; then you will be able to use it in some of the recipes that call for the Cream Soup Mix. A few recipes use cheese, cream cheese, or sour cream; these are not milk free.

Almond meal is listed as a substitute for dry milk powder in a few recipes. If both milk and almond are a problem for your needs, you can make these recipes omitting the dry milk and the almond meal. You can use rice or soy milk in place of the water. Just know the product will be a little less moist and not last quite as long.

All the recipes that call for butter can be made successfully with a nondairy margarine like Nucoa or shortening in place of the butter.

Premeasured Mixes

One trick that I have found to be most helpful is to premeasure the dry ingredients of the recipes I use often. I put the dry ingredients into reusable containers and label them with the wet ingredients needed to complete the recipe. Then I have a pantry full of ready-to-use pancake mix, waffle mix, pizza crust mix, etc. I find I am more likely to cook with the ready-to-go mixes done this way. I usually find a quiet moment (when the kids are at school) and measure out the dry ingredients for a couple weeks' worth of mixes. This one trick has made my life so much easier I just couldn't help but share it with you. (Caution, don't put brown sugar in the mixes until you add wet ingredients; it will harden while sitting with the other dry ingredients.)

Double Batches

I often make a double batch of whatever I am cooking and freeze the second batch to use later. This makes it possible to have a few quick, ready-made meals. Most of the recipes in this book freeze well (cinnamon rolls don't do so well; they are an exception.)

Adaptation

I have offered some basic recipes in this book in hopes that you can use them to adapt recipes your family already loves. I recommend you use these recipes to make a new gluten free version of your family favorites, or recipes you find online or in other cookbooks. The Cream Soup Mix is a great substitute for canned cream of chicken or cream of mushroom soup. The graham crackers crushed make a great graham cracker pie crust. Most recipes that call for flour you can substitute the same amount of UNflour plus a teaspoon or so of xanthan gum and they turn out great. The possibilities are as endless as your sense of adventure in cooking.

School Lunch

School lunch for a child on a gluten-free diet can be difficult. I have worked out a system with my children's school, because I just don't expect the lunch ladies to really understand how to stay gluten free. So I send lunch with my kids every day. I have arranged to have a microwave in the classroom that my child has access to. I send leftovers in glass containers with lids that can be heated up and taken to the lunch room. When I make the bread recipe from this book I slice one loaf and freeze it for sandwiches anytime. And my kids' favorite is a pancake sandwich. I spend a day making a triple batch of pancakes, then put a precooked sausage patty between two pancakes, put them in a ziplock bag and then in the freezer. My kids love it, and I love the ease on those busy mornings.

Gluten-Free Vacations

Going on a trip can be a whole new adventure when eating gluten free. Here are some ways we have made it work: We try to stay at a resort with a kitchen, or rent a cabin or beach house with a fully supplied kitchen. Before the trip I plan a menu for each day, make a grocery list of the things I can buy anywhere, and pack the special foods necessary. The first day of the vacation I go to the grocery store and buy the things on my list. I go with the least stressful meals possible, preparing anything ahead of time that I can. We always take a cooler in the car for the perishables. There are many chain restaurants that have websites that list any gluten-free options they have. We always print off a few to have with us so that we can eat on the road when possible.

And just to let you know, Disneyland has added gluten-free options in all their restaurants in the park. Yea for Disney!

Emotional Support

Check in your city for a Gluten Intolerance Group. These groups are great for learning information, as the gluten-free world is always changing. And it is nice to have some friends who really understand what it takes to be a gluten-free cook! Hats off to my GIG, they are my heroes!!

UNflour

In *Alice in Wonderland*, every day that is **not your birthday** is called your "**un-birthday.**" Because the **flour** I use throughout this cookbook is made from *gluten-free* ingredients, I am going to borrow a trick from the **Mad Hatter** and call it "UNflour." And, as you will soon find out, cooking with UNflour is a *party*, every day.

Ingredients

for Small Batch

3 cups rice flour (brown or white)
2 ½ cups cornstarch
1 ½ cups tapioca flour

for Medium Batch

6 cups rice flour (brown or white)
5 cups cornstarch
3 cups tapioca flour

for Large Batch

9 cups rice flour (brown or white)
7 ½ cups cornstarch
4 ½ cups tapioca flour

Special Note
UNflour is used throughout this book.

Directions

1. Choose what size batch UNflour you want to make. Put all ingredients into an air tight container, mix well.

Throughout the book, anytime the ingredients call for UNflour, it is referring to the mix on this page.

I keep five-quart ice cream buckets and use them to mix and store UNflour. The medium batch fits perfectly into the ice cream bucket. I just measure it out, snap the lid on tight, and shake to mix.

Most grocery stores carry these three ingredients. Look for a health food section and you will most likely find them. I use UNflour so often that I buy these three ingredients in bulk. Check with a health food store or grocery store near you to order 25 lb bags of each flour. It will fit nicely in a typical white storage bucket. White rice flour will last many months with no refrigeration needed. Brown rice flour is best stored in a cool place.

When shopping for Tapioca Flour, keep in mind that Tapioca Flour and Tapioca Starch are the same thing.

Cream Soup Mix

This **Cream Soup Mix** can be used to replace *cream of chicken* or *cream of mushroom soup* in many recipes. Use it in **casseroles**, as **gravy**, or just to make your favorite kind of cream soup.

Ingredients

for Small Batch

2 cups instant dry milk
¾ cups cornstarch
¼ cup gluten-free chicken bouillon powder
½ teaspoon pepper
½ teaspoon thyme
½ teaspoon tarragon

for Medium Batch

4 cups instant dry milk
1 ½ cups cornstarch
½ cup gluten-free chicken bouillon powder
1 teaspoon pepper
1 teaspoon thyme
1 teaspoon tarragon

for Large Batch

8 cups instant dry milk
3 cups cornstarch
1 cup gluten-free chicken bouillon powder
2 teaspoons pepper
2 teaspoons thyme
2 teaspoons tarragon

Directions

1. Choose what size batch **Cream Soup Mix** you want to make. Put all ingredients into an airtight container, mix well.

Store this **Cream Soup Mix** at room temperature. Refer to "best if used by" dates on powdered milk for accurate shelf life.

To make the equivilant of 1 can of soup:

Ingredients

⅓ cup **Cream Soup Mix**
1 cup cold water

Directions

In a saucepan combine **Cream Soup Mix** and cold water. Stirring constantly, heat over medium heat until soup thickens and begins to boil.

See recipes in this book that use **Cream Soup Mix**:

IrresistiblyGlutenFree: Simple Family Favorite Re

Bread

If you have a **child** that was *picky* before the diagnosis, then you are probably feeling *hopeless* by now. Well, here's a **loaf** of *hope*. Even **my pickiest kid** loves this Bread! And if you have never made Bread before, don't worry; this Bread is quite **simple** to make.

Ingredients

Dry

3 ½ cups UNflour (see page 12)
½ cup instant dry milk
   (or almond meal)
2 tablespoons sugar
2 teaspoons xanthan gum
¾ teaspoon salt
2 teaspoons baking powder
1 tablespoon instant dry yeast

Wet

1 ½ cups warm water
4 tablespoons butter slightly
   softened or shortening
2 eggs

If you want to cut this recipe in half to make one loaf of bread, don't reduce the yeast. You will still need 1 tablespoon of yeast for one loaf. The recipe for Rolls is the same as one loaf, see page 18.

Directions

1. Grease two 8½ x 4½-inch bread pans. (Flouring is not necessary and only makes the bread gritty.)

2. Combine dry ingredients in mixer.

3. While mixing on low add warm water, butter, and eggs. Beat on high for 2-3 minutes. (This dough thins as it beats; by the time you have beaten it for 2-3 minutes it should be like an extra thick cake batter. Use more or less water to get the right consistency.)

4. Spread dough into prepared pans. Cover loosely with plastic wrap sprayed with cooking spray. Let rise until double in size (about 30 to 40 minutes).

5. Remove plastic wrap and bake in preheated oven at 365 degrees for 50 to 60 minutes, covered loosely with aluminum foil after the first 10 minutes.

6. After removing bread from oven, remove from pans to prevent a soggy bottom. Butter tops if desired. Let bread cool a little before slicing.

I like to use almond meal instead of instant dry milk, as it keeps the bread moist longer and increases nutritional value. You can make almond meal by grinding whole almonds in a food processor or grinder.

Rolls

This is the *same recipe* as the **bread recipe**, just *cut in half* and **adjusted** to make Rolls.

Ingredients

Dry
1 ¾ cups UNflour (see page 12)
¼ cup instant dry milk
   (or almond meal)
1 tablespoon sugar
1 teaspoon xanthan gum
½ teaspoon salt
1 teaspoon baking powder
1 tablespoon instant dry yeast

Wet
¾ cup warm water
2 tablespoons butter slightly
   softened or shortening
1 egg

You can also use the bread recipe to make approximately 20 rolls or one loaf of bread and 10 rolls.

Directions

1. Grease muffin tin or spray with cooking spray.
2. Combine dry ingredients in mixer.
3. While mixing on low add warm water, butter, and egg. Beat on high for 2-3 minutes. (Dough will thin as it mixes; it should end up like a thick cake batter.)
4. Fill each muffin cup a little over halfway by spooning in dough.
5. Wet fingers and lightly smooth the top of each roll for a nice rounded top.
6. Spray plastic wrap with cooking spray and cover rolls. Set in warm place for 20 minutes to rise. (Rolls should double in size.)
7. Remove plastic wrap. Bake in preheated oven at 365 degrees for about 20 minutes.
8. After removing rolls from oven, remove from muffin tin to prevent soggy bottoms. Butter tops if desired. Makes about 10 rolls.

IrresistiblyGlutenFree: Simple Family Favorite Re

Hamburger Buns

Gluten-free bread dough is *too thin and sticky* to roll out like *wheat dough*. For the longest time I could not figure out a way to make things like Hamburger Buns. Then one day *it hit me*, since I can't shape the dough, find a **container** that does the shaping for me. I keep **large tuna fish cans**, and they do the job just fine.

Ingredients

Dry
1 ¾ cups UNflour (see page 12)
¼ cup instant dry milk
   (or almond meal)
1 tablespoon sugar
1 teaspoon xanthan gum
½ teaspoon salt
1 teaspoon baking powder
1 tablespoon instant dry yeast

Wet
¾ cup warm water
2 tablespoons butter slightly
   softened or shortening
1 egg

You can use this same recipe with regular tuna fish cans to make small hamburger buns, or larger rolls, or breakfast egg and sausage muffins.

Directions

1. Prepare 6 emptied and cleaned large tuna cans (or 12.5 oz chicken cans) with cooking spray.

2. Combine dry ingredients in mixer.

3. While mixing on low add warm water, butter, and egg. Beat on high for 2-3 minutes. (Dough will thin as it mixes; it should end up like a thick cake batter.)

4. Put approximately ⅓ cup dough in the bottom of each can.

5. Wet fingers and lightly smooth the top of each bun for a nice rounded top.

6. Cover loosely with plastic wrap and let rise for 30 minutes, or until about double in size.

7. Remove plastic wrap. Bake in preheated oven at 360 degrees for about 20 minutes or until tops are golden brown and bread springs back when pressed with fingers.

8. Remove from cans immediately after taking out of oven to prevent soggy bottoms. Once buns are cooled, cut in half to form the top and bottom bun.

Pizza

This **Pizza** dough is spread, almost *like frosting*, on the bottom of a pan. And it *really sticks* to the pan. I have found it best to use **9-inch round silicone bakeware**. The crust *doesn't* stick, and you *don't* have to **grease** it, which makes **spreading much easier**.

Ingredients

Dry

1 ¼ cups **UNflour** (see page 12)
¼ cup cornstarch
¼ cup tapioca flour
1 teaspoon xanthan gum
¼ cup Instant dry milk
   (or almond meal)
1 teaspoon sugar
½ teaspoon salt or onion salt
1 teaspoon baking powder
1 tablespoon instant dry yeast

Wet

1 cup warm water (plus or minus)
2 tablespoons shortening
1 egg

This crust is also good to use as breadsticks; just top with butter and garlic salt!

Directions

1. Combine all dry ingredients (including yeast) in bowl of heavy mixer.

2. While mixing on low add water, shortening, and egg. Beat on high for 2 minutes. (This dough thins as it mixes; it starts out like a thin cookie dough, but should look like a thick cake batter when done mixing.)

3. Divide dough into three 9-inch silicone pans. Spread dough to evenly coat the bottom of each pan.

4. Put in oven and turn on to 375 degrees.

5. Bake for 15 minutes. This includes the preheat time. (The dough will rise while the oven is preheating.)

6. Transfer crusts to cookie sheets. Top with sauce, cheese, and favorite toppings. (I use a gluten-free spaghetti sauce.)

7. Bake an additional 15-20 minutes, or until cheese, is melted and slightly bubbly on top.

Make extra crusts. These untopped crusts freeze well and are fantastic for quick snacks or meals. Just top them frozen and add 5 minutes to the baking time.

Corn Bread

This is a **really good** Corn Bread that stays **moist** for *days*.
A **happy compliment** to almost any meal.

Ingredients

Dry
1 cup UNflour (see page 12)
1 cup cornmeal
½ teaspoon xanthan gum
¼ cup sugar
1 teaspoon salt
1 teaspoon baking powder
1 teaspoon baking soda

Wet
1 cup applesauce
2 eggs
2 tablespoons butter or
    margarine softened
¼ cup water

Directions

1. Preheat oven to 375 degrees.
2. Place dry ingredients in bowl of mixer.
3. While mixing on low add wet ingredients. Mix for 30 seconds.
4. Pour batter into greased 8-inch square pan.
5. Bake for 25 minutes or until it tests done with a toothpick.
6. Serve with honey or jam. Double recipe for 9x13 pan.

If you are avoiding eggs; this recipe works without eggs; just add an extra ¼ cup applesauce instead of eggs.

This corn bread also works with plain yogurt in place of applesauce.

Muffins

Choose your **favorite** kind of Muffin and *enjoy!*

Ingredients

Dry

1 ½ cups UNflour (see page 12)
¾ teaspoon xanthan gum
½ cup sugar
½ teaspoon salt
1 ½ teaspoons baking powder
¼ teaspoon baking soda

Wet

¾ cup milk (or milk substitute)
1 egg
4 tablespoons butter slightly softened

Directions

1. Choose the type of muffin you want to make from the choices below. Preheat oven to 350 degrees.
2. Combine dry ingredients in bowl of mixer.
3. While mixing on low add wet ingredients and any additional ingredients according to your muffin choice below. Mix on high 1 minute.
4. Fill greased muffin cups (or tins lined with cupcake papers) just over half full.
5. Bake at 350 degrees for about 30 minutes or until muffin tests clean with a toothpick.

Makes 12 muffins.

Blueberry Muffins

Add ½ cup dried blueberries or ½ cup canned blueberry pie filling and only ⅓ cup of the milk.

Apple Cinnamon Muffins

Add ½ teaspoon cinnamon and 1 apple peeled and grated.

Banana Muffins

Add 1 small, ripe banana mashed.

Lemon Poppyseed Muffins

Replace the milk with a 6 oz cup of lemon yogurt (or ¾ cup lemon yogurt) and add 2 teaspoons poppyseeds, a 2.9 oz package of lemon cook and serve pudding mix, and ¼ cup lemon juice.

Waffles

All of my kids love these Waffles! I use a Belgian waffle iron for fantastic Waffles. For a special treat, serve with **strawberry jam** or **strawberries** and **whipped cream**. Or just eat them *plain*; they **taste great**, even *without syrup*!

Ingredients

Dry

1 ½ cups UNflour (see page 12)
¼ teaspoon xanthan gum
2 tablespoons sugar
½ teaspoon salt
1 ¼ teaspoons baking powder
¼ teaspoon ground cinnamon

Wet

½ teaspoon vanilla
¾ cups milk (or milk substitute)
2 eggs
¼ cup canola or vegetable oil

Directions

1. Place dry ingredients in bowl of mixer.
2. While mixing, add milk, eggs, and oil. Beat on high for 2 minutes.
3. Follow the directions for your waffle iron and pour recommended amount of batter onto lightly greased iron. Cook for recommended time as well, should be golden brown when done.

Makes eight 4-inch waffles.

These waffles freeze well, so you may want to make some extras to eat later. Just reheat each frozen waffle in the microwave for 30-40 seconds, or toast in the toaster.

Pancakes

I made these Pancakes **for my Dad** (the first diagnosed celiac in my family) **and he thought they were no different** from the *wheat infested* Pancakes he had always loved. That was my moment of *triumph!*

Ingredients

Dry
1 cup UNflour (see page 12)
½ cup cornstarch
½ teaspoon xanthan gum
¼ cup sugar
½ teaspoon salt
1 teaspoon baking powder
½ teaspoon baking soda

Wet
1 cup milk (or milk substitute)
¼ cup canola or vegetable oil
2 eggs

To keep each pancake golden brown and even colored, remove pan from burner between each pancake, pour the new batter on, then return to burner.

Directions

1. Place dry ingredients in bowl of mixer.
2. While mixing on low add milk, oil and eggs. Beat on high to remove any lumps.
3. Pour ⅛ to ¼ cup batter onto heated griddle. (If you do them too big they will not cook all the way through before they burn.)
4. Using the bottom of your measuring cup (or a spoon) spread batter in a circle to about ⅛ inch thick.
5. Once bubbles are popping all over the top of the pancake, turn over and cook the other side about a minute. (Keep temperature at medium-low to prevent burning.)
6. Serve with syrup, jam, or whatever you like.

Makes 16-18 pancakes.

Crepes

These **Crepes** are *so easy* to make and work great for **breakfast** or for your favorite **dinner** recipe.

Ingredients

Dry
¼ cup UNflour (see page 12)
½ teaspoon salt

Wet
¼ teaspoon vanilla
3 eggs
¼ cup milk (or milk substitute)

Directions

1. Combine all ingredients in mixing bowl and mix on high to remove all lumps.

2. Heat a small frying pan on medium heat and coat with cooking spray.

3. Pour a little less than ¼ cup batter into pan. (I like to use the same ¼ cup measuring cup that I used for measuring ingredients and fill it just less than full.)

4. Swish the pan around to cover the pan with batter and get crepe into a nice, round shape.

5. Turn over after one minute or so and cook other side for about half a minute.

6. Fill with jam, syrup, or fruit, fold over and sprinkle top with powdered sugar. Or fill with chicken and top with gravy for a chicken-stuffed-crepe dinner.

Makes six 6-inch crepes.

Tea Party Quiche

What **little girl** doesn't love a *tea party?*
These are **cute** and **yummy!** I save the *heels* of my
gluten-free bread in the freezer and cut them up to use
in this recipe.

Ingredients

8 eggs
1 ½ teaspoons dried onion flakes
   (or 2 teaspoons finely diced
   onion)
1 ½ cups milk (or milk substitute)
⅛ teaspoon paprika
⅛ teaspoon onion salt (or regular
   salt if desired)
⅛ teaspoon pepper
8 ounces ground sausage
1 ounce grated cheddar cheese
4 slices gluten-free bread cut into
   small cubes (or 1 cup gluten-free
   hash browns)

Directions

1. Preheat oven to 325 degrees. Grease muffin tin well.

2. Cook the ground sausage and drain grease.

3. Beat eggs well. Mix eggs, milk, onion flakes, and
   seasonings, preferably in something with a spout for
   easier pouring.

4. In the bottom of each muffin cup put 1 tablespoon
   of each: sausage, bread, and cheese.

5. Pour egg mixture into each muffin cup until it reaches
   the top and covers the other ingredients.

6. Bake for 45 minutes. Run a knife around the edges
   of each quiche and then remove when cooled
   10 minutes.

Makes 12 quiches.

Chicken Nuggets

If your **child** has been *missing* their favorite restaurant **Chicken Nuggets**, here you go. These are **pretty darn close** to what you find in a *kids meal*.

Ingredients

4 chicken breasts cut into nugget-size pieces

Batter

1 cup UNflour (see page 12)
½ teaspoon xanthan gum
1 teaspoon Emeril's Original Essence (or seasoning salt of your choice)
¼ teaspoon pepper
⅔ cup water

For cooking

2 cups canola or vegetable oil

Directions

1. Cook cubed chicken in frying pan until no longer pink, rinse off any fat and remove to paper towel, pat off any excess water, set aside.

2. Heat canola oil on medium-high in a deep frying pan (or use a deep fryer at about 300 degrees).

3. In a bowl mix the batter ingredients.

4. Dip each piece of chicken into batter and fully coat, then drop in hot oil. (I usually do about 5 or 6 at a time in the oil.)

5. Cook each piece about a minute on each side, then remove from oil using a slotted spoon and place on paper towel.

6. Repeat this process until all chicken has been cooked. Cool and enjoy.

Macaroni & Cheese

It appears there are a few different types of Macaroni and Cheese, and to **my kids**, there is a *vast difference* between them. Here are some **ideas** to help you find the Mac and Cheese **your child** likes *best*.

Ingredients

Macaroni...

1 package gluten-free macaroni elbows (I recommend Tinkya'da brand pastas)

Prepare according to directions. I like to add the 1 tablespoon canola oil to the boiling water to help keep the macaroni from sticking together.

and Cheese

1 can evaporated milk
½ cup chicken broth
3 tablespoons cornstarch
1 tablespoon mustard
2 cups grated extra-sharp cheddar cheese

Directions

1. In saucepan combine milk, broth, cornstarch, and mustard.
2. While stirring, bring to a boil over medium heat.
3. Add in grated cheese and stir until melted.
4. Mix in cooked gluten-free macaroni and serve.

Or

1. Use the powdered cheese packet from a regular box of mac and cheese and follow directions for mixing cheese, save the wheat macaroni in a large ziplock bag to use for a gluten eater, or donate to a friend or food bank. Be sure and check the cheese packet ingredients and ensure it is gluten free.

If you don't want "stringy" cheese, add ¼ teaspoon lemon juice to cheese sauce, stir.

Corn Dogs

My **boys** have been longing for a Corn Dog for years. I was so *happy* when I finally figured out a way to make them. These are really quite **easy** to make and are not *greasy*, because they are **baked**.

Ingredients

8 gluten-free hot dogs
8 kebob skewers

Dry

¾ cup UNflour (see page 12)
¾ cup cornmeal
1 ½ teaspoons xanthan gum
¼ cup sugar
½ teaspoon salt
1 teaspoons baking powder

Wet

¼ cup milk (or milk substitute)
1 egg
6 tablespoons butter slightly
    softened

To make step 5 easier, I also sprinkle a dusting of cornstarch on the top of the dough and pat to an even thickness, then cut it into 8 parts with a knife.

Directions

1. Combine all dry and wet ingredients in bowl of heavy mixer. Mix on low for 1 minute.

2. Continue mixing for an additional 3 minutes on high to remove lumps. Dough will be thick, but sticky.

3. Cut the bottom 3 inches or so off each skewer to make appropriate length stick. Be sure to cut the pointed end off for safety reasons.

4. Push one end of the skewer just past halfway up the hot dog, keeping the skewer as much in the middle of the hot dog as possible.

5. Dust countertop with cornstarch. Scrape dough onto dusted countertop. Divide into 8 equal parts.

6. With your hands dusted with cornstarch, take ⅛ of the dough and pat around a hot dog as evenly as possible. Repeat for each hot dog.

7. Place the corn dogs on a cookie sheet lined with aluminum foil (for easy clean up). Roll each dog back and forth on the foil to smooth it out. Make sure the hot dogs are not touching.

8. Bake in oven preheated to 350 degrees for about 30 minutes. To bake evenly, roll each corn dog every 10 minutes.

Makes 8 corn dogs.

IrresistiblyGlutenFree: Simple Family Favorite R

Lemon Chicken

This is like the Lemon Chicken you would find in a **Chinese restaurant**.
You can also **experiment** with **other sauces**, or see if the sauces at your local
Chinese restaurant are *gluten free* and use them for an **almost-take-out dinner**.
It uses the same recipe as the **chicken nuggets**.

Ingredients

4 chicken breasts

Batter

1 cup UNflour (see page 12)
½ teaspoon xanthan gum
1 teaspoon Emeril's Original Essence
   (or seasoning salt of your choice)
¼ teaspoon pepper
¾ cup water

For cooking

2 cups canola or vegetable oil

Sauce

1 can (14 oz) chicken broth
   (about 2 cups)
1 lemon (you will be using the
   juice and the peel)
¼ teaspoon garlic powder
1 cup sugar
3 tablespoons cornstarch
¼ cup water

Directions

1. Cut chicken breasts into bite-size pieces. Cook in frying pan until no longer pink, rinse off any fat and remove to paper towel, pat off any excess water, set aside.

2. Heat canola oil on medium-high in a deep frying pan (or use a deep fryer at about 300 degrees).

3. In a bowl mix the batter ingredients.

4. Dip each piece of chicken into batter and fully coat, then drop in hot oil. I usually do about 5 or 6 at a time in the oil.

5. Cook each piece about a minute on each side, then remove from oil using a slotted spoon and place on paper towel.

6. Repeat this process until all chicken has been cooked. Set aside.

8. For sauce, put broth, sugar and garlic powder in a saucepan. Finely grate ½ of the lemon's peel and add to the broth, then cut the lemon and squeeze the juice out into the sauce.

9. In a cup, mix the cornstarch and ¼ cup water and stir to remove lumps. While heating sauce on medium heat, add cornstarch and water mixture, stirring constantly until sauce comes to a boil and thickens.

11. Serve chicken on rice and top with lemon sauce.

Orange Chicken

This was my **favorite childhood recipe**. I remember *begging* my mom to make it. Years after the recipe *was lost* I began working to try and **recreate** the Orange Chicken I remembered. I am **happy** to share it with you now.

Ingredients

4 chicken breasts
1 cup frozen orange juice concentrate
¼ cup dijon mustard
⅓ cup brown sugar
2 tablespoons gluten-free soy sauce
2 tablespoons canola or vegetable oil
¼ teaspoon black pepper
3 tablespoons cornstarch
¼ cup cold water

Directions

1. In a slow cooker put chicken, orange juice, mustard, sugar, soy sauce, oil and pepper.
2. Cook on low for about 6 hours, or until chicken is starting to fall apart. (Or bake in the oven for 1 hour in a baking dish if you don't want to use a slow cooker.)
3. Remove chicken from slow cooker. Pour the remaining drippings through a colander and into a saucepan.
4. In a cup, mix the cornstarch and cold water until fully mixed, leaving no lumps.
5. Pour the cornstarch mixture into the saucepan with the chicken drippings.
6. Heat on medium heat, stirring constantly until sauce starts to boil and thicken.
7. Return chicken and sauce to the slow cooker for about ½ hour, or until ready to serve.
8. Serve the chicken over rice and top with the orange sauce.

Chicken Casserole

Here is an *easy* meal you can **make ahead** and pop in the oven to heat before dinnertime. My **kids** like this Chicken Casserole because the *vegetables* are **not mixed in**. (Apparently that makes them "gross.")

Ingredients

4 cups cooked rice

1 can (12.5 oz.) of chunked chicken breast (or 2 chicken breasts cooked and chopped)

1 lb ground sausage

1 tablespoon dried onion flakes

⅔ cup Cream Soup Mix with 2 cups water (see page 14)

½ cup sour cream

Directions

1. Cook and drain sausage.

2. Coat a 9x13 baking dish with cooking spray. Preheat oven to 350 degrees.

3. Spread cooked rice in the baking dish.

4. Top rice with chunked chicken, cooked sausage and onion flakes, set aside.

5. In a saucepan combine Cream Soup Mix and cold water. Stirring constantly, heat over medium heat until soup thickens and begins to boil.

6. Add sour cream to soup and stir well to remove lumps.

7. Pour soup over the other ingredients in baking dish. Cover casserole with aluminum foil.

8. Heat in oven at 350 degrees for about 1 hour.

9. Serve with vegetables of your choice, *on the side!*

Italian Chicken

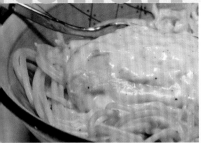

When we take dinner to the **neighbors** we usually take them Italian Chicken. It is a **mild-enough-for-kids** but **tasty-enough-for-adults** white sauce that everyone wants the recipe for.

Ingredients

4 chicken breasts
2 tablespoons melted butter
1 packet Italian salad dressing and recipe mix
⅔ cup Cream Soup Mix (see page 14)
2 cups water
1 8 oz package cream cheese

The chicken should be fall-apart-tender, so it mixes into the sauce. Or you can carefully remove the chicken and serve them as whole chicken breasts. We love to put the sauce over steamed vegetables too.

Directions

1. Put butter, Italian seasoning packet, and chicken in slow cooker.

2. Cook on low for 5-6 hours.

3. In a saucepan combine Cream Soup Mix and cold water. Stirring constantly, heat over medium heat until soup thickens and begins to boil.

4. Add cream cheese to cream soup and stir well. (If you don't want any lumps, beat with electric mixer until smooth.)

5. Remove any fat that has separated from the chicken while cooking, but keep the rest of the juices. (I use a colander and strain the juices and then return them to the slow cooker with the chicken.)

6. Pour the cream cheese and soup mixture into the slow cooker with the chicken and juices.

7. Stir, and cook on low for another 2 hours.

8. Serve over rice or gluten-free pasta.

This can be cooked in the oven instead of the slow cooker. Follow the same directions, but cook on 350 degrees for 1 hour before adding the soup sauce and then ½ hour more after adding the soup sauce. It will not be as fall-apart, but still good.

Hawaiian Haystacks

A *gluten-free diet* often means loss of choices. Hawaiian Haystacks is a **fun** dinner that lets you make some **choices**. Set out a smorgasbord of toppings and build **dinner** *your way*.

Ingredients

⅔ cup Cream Soup Mix and
   2 cups water (see page 14)
¼ cup sour cream
1 can (12.5 oz.) of canned chicken,
   heated
1 can pineapple tidbits, drained
1 can mandarin oranges, drained
2 medium tomatoes diced
2 green onions chopped
1 cup peas heated
Flaked coconut (to taste)
Chopped nuts of choice

Directions

1. In a saucepan combine Cream Soup Mix and cold water. Stirring constantly, heat over medium heat until soup thickens and begins to boil.

2. Add sour cream to soup, stir well to mix.

3. Start your stack with rice on the bottom, then add whatever you like on top, including sauce. Every haystack is a little different, just like every person!

Enchilada Casserole

This is a recipe I use on **busy days**. I make the Enchilada Casserole early in the day (when the kids are at school) and just pop it in the oven an **hour before dinner**. Then I can help the kids with *homework* and still eat dinner at a *decent hour!*

Ingredients

12 white corn tortillas
1 lb. hamburger (or chicken)
2 lbs shredded cheese
1 19-ounce can mild enchilada
    sauce red or green
⅔ cup Cream Soup Mix with
    2 cups water (see page 14)

We prefer the red enchilada sauce and hamburger together, and the green chilli enchilada sauce with chicken.

Directions

1. Cook and drain hamburger (or chicken), set aside.

2. In a saucepan combine Cream Soup Mix and cold water. Stirring constantly, heat over medium heat until soup thickens and begins to boil.

3. Pour enchilada sauce into soup and stir until well mixed.

4. Prepare a 9x13 baking dish by spraying with cooking spray. Preheat oven to 350 degrees.

5. Take four tortillas and one by one dip both sides in the enchilada sauce mixture and lay in the bottom of the baking dish.

6. Top with ⅓ of the cooked hamburger (or chicken) and ⅓ of the grated cheese.

7. Dip the next four tortillas and place on top.

8. Continue layering dipped tortillas with the meat and cheese until all are used.

9. Cover casserole with aluminum foil and bake at 350 degrees for 1 hour.

10. Allow to cool, cut into squares, serve with sour cream if desired.

Smothered Meatballs

This is a great recipe to get the **kids involved!** My **6-year-old** loves to roll the Meatballs. And you can lighten up the Meatballs with a variety of *healthy choices*.

Ingredients

Meatballs
2 lbs ground beef
½ packet onion soup mix
   (check labels for gluten free)
2 eggs
¼ cup ketchup
1 cup gluten-free bread crumbs
   (or steamed and pureed veggies)

Sauce
1 cup Cream Soup Mix
   (see page 14)
3 cups water
1 cup sour cream
½ cup milk
2 tablespoons Worchestershire sauce
   (check labels for gluten free)

Directions

1. In heavy mixer, combine ground beef, onion soup mix, eggs, ketchup, bread crumbs (or veggies), salt and pepper. Mix well.

2. Roll meat mixture into small, bite-sized meatballs, and place on a cookie sheet or baking pan lined with aluminum foil. (The foil makes for easy clean up!)

3. Bake in oven preheated to 350 degrees for 1 hour.

4. In a saucepan combine Cream Soup Mix and cold water. Stirring constantly, heat over medium heat until soup thickens and begins to boil.

5. Add sour cream, milk and Worchestershire sauce, stir well.

6. Add cooked meatballs to sauce and stir together.

7. Serve smothered meatballs over gluten-free pasta or rice.

If your family likes both of the meatball recipes in this book try doubling the meatball batch and freezing half to use for the other recipe later.

I like to put steamed and pureed carrots or squash in the meatballs rather than bread crumbs. A sneaky little trick to get 'em more veggies!

54

Sweet & Sour Meatballs

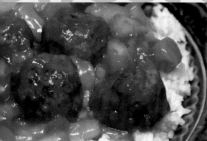

Sweet & Sour Meatballs is an absolute *favorite dinner* with my **kids**. It does take a ***little more time*** than most of my recipes, so it is met with **great excitement** when they **smell it cooking!**

Ingredients

Meatballs

2 lbs ground beef
½ packet onion soup mix
   (check labels for gluten free)
2 eggs
¼ cup ketchup
1 cup gluten-free bread crumbs
   (or steamed and pureed veggies)
2 large carrots sliced
2 cloves garlic, minced
1 can (20 oz) pineapple tidbits
   (save juice)

Sauce

Reserved juice from pineapple
   tidbits
1 can (6-ounce) pineapple juice
2 tablespoons cornstarch
⅓ cup brown sugar
2 tablespoons gluten-free soy sauce
¼ cup lemon juice
½ cup ketchup
¼ teaspoon ground ginger

Directions

1. In heavy mixer, combine ground beef, onion soup mix, eggs, ketchup, bread crumbs (or veggies), salt and pepper. Mix well.

2. Roll meat mixture into small, bite-sized meatballs, and place on a cookie sheet or baking pan lined with aluminum foil. (The foil makes for easy clean up!)

3. Bake in oven preheated to 350 degrees for 1 hour.

4. Stir fry carrots and garlic together until just starting to soften, set aside.

5. Mix sauce ingredients together, stir well, set aside.

6. In a large pot, or deep frying pan, combine cooked meatballs, carrots, and pineapple tidbits.

7. Pour in sauce while stirring on medium heat until sauce thickens and comes to a boil.

8. Serve over rice.

You can make this recipe with cooked and cubed chicken instead of meatballs. It is still very good, but my family prefers it with meatballs.

Sloppy Joes

We have a "rice" version of Sloppy Joes in honor of Jackie Chan. We call it *"Sloppy Chan."* Before I figured out how to make **hamburger buns** we developed this **family favorite recipe** and put the Sloppy Joes sauce over **rice**. You can choose which style your family likes best.

Ingredients

4-6 hamburger buns (see page 20) or 4-6 cups cooked rice

2 lbs ground beef

Sauce

1 cup water

3 tablespoons cornstarch

¼ cup Worchestershire sauce (check labels for gluten free)

3 tablespoons brown sugar

2 tablespoons vinegar (such as apple cider or rice vinegar)

2 teaspoons mustard

1 cup ketchup

½ small onion minced (or 1 tablespoons dried onion flakes)

Directions

1. Cook and drain ground beef. Set aside.

2. Stir sauce ingredients together leaving no lumps.

2. Add sauce to cooked ground beef, stirring constantly over medium heat until sauce thickens and boils.

3. Serve on buns or over rice.

To make less mess while mixing the sauce, I use a glass, 4-cup measuring cup. I add each ingredient to the same cup, watching it rise to the amount required. Then I stir and pour it right from the measuring cup into the pan with the hamburger.

Chocolate Chip Cookies

These are **light** and **fluffy**, cake-like Chocolate Chip Cookies, and boy do they *melt in your mouth*.

Ingredients

Dry

1 ¼ cups UNflour (see page 12)
½ teaspoon xanthan gum
¾ cup brown sugar
½ teaspoon salt
¼ teaspoon baking soda

Wet

⅓ cup water
2 egg yolks
1 teaspoon vanilla
½ cup (1 cube) butter or
   margarine slightly softened
1 cup chocolate chips (or ½ cup
   chocolate and ½ cup
   butterscotch chips)

To slightly soften butter, just put it in the microwave for 5 seconds, then turn it over and do another 5 seconds on the other side.

Directions

1. Preheat oven to 350 degrees.
2. In bowl of heavy mixer combine all dry ingredients.
3. While mixing on low add wet ingredients, and end with chocolate chips.
4. Scrape cookie dough into a container and place in refrigerator for about 2 hours.

If you don't want to wait the 2 hours to chill, you can put the dough directly into a greased 9x9 baking dish, sheet cookie style, and bake at 350 degrees for about 15-20 min and cut into squares when cool.

5. Using a large spoon, drop dough by spoonfuls onto greased cookie sheet.
6. Bake for about 12 minutes.
   Makes 2 dozen cookies.

Sugar Cookies

My **unsuspecting neighbor** got into these Sugar Cookies one day not knowing they were *gluten free*. He liked them so much he asked his wife to **get the recipe** from me.
I love fooling wheat-eaters!

Ingredients

Dry

1 ¾ cup UNflour (see page 12)
1 teaspoon xanthan gum
⅔ cup sugar
½ tsp salt

Wet

½ cup (one cube) butter or
    margarine slightly softened
2 egg yolks
1 teaspoon vanilla
½ teaspoon butter (or lemon)
    flavored extract
3 tablespoons water

If dough is sticky and hard to work with, try adding a bit more UNflour, or try placing it in the refrigerator for one or two hours first.

Directions

1. Put dry ingredients in bowl of mixer.

2. While mixing on low add butter, egg yolks, water, and extracts.

3. Mix on high, dough will be quite stiff.

4. Dust clean counter and rolling pin with cornstarch and roll dough to about ¼ inch thick.

5. Cut into desired shape with cookie cutter and place on greased baking sheet.

6. Bake in oven preheated to 350 degrees for about 15 minutes.

7. These cookies look about the same color coming out as they do going in, so you have to check the bottom of one for a slight browning to know when they are done. They also feel very soft in the oven; they firm up as they cool.

8. Remove from cookie sheet and cool. Frost and sprinkle if desired. (If you don't like frosting, you can top cookies with colored sugar or sprinkles before you bake them.)

Makes 2 dozen cookies.

Brownies

The **melted chocolate chips** in this recipe give the Brownies that **gooey, fudgy taste** you *love* in a Brownie. If you don't like that **gooey, fudgy taste,** just leave them out; you'll have a nice cake-like Brownie.

Ingredients

Dry

1 ¼ cups UNflour (see page 12)
1 teaspoon xanthan gum
1 ¼ cups sugar
½ teaspoon salt
1 teaspoon baking powder
¾ cup cocoa

Wet

1 cup milk (or milk substitute)
2 eggs
1 tsp vanilla
½ cup (1 cube) butter softened
1 ½ cups chocolate chips or butterscotch chips melted (Microwave in a glass bowl for about 2 min, stirring after the first minute.)

Directions

1. Preheat oven to 350 degrees.
2. Place all dry ingredients in mixer.
3. While mixing on low add milk, eggs, butter, and melted chocolate chips.
4. Mix well on medium speed.
5. Pour batter into greased 9x13 pan.
6. Bake for 35 minutes.
7. Cool before serving.

Chocolate Cake

Happy Birthday! How fun is it to make a *gluten-free* Chocolate Cake that doesn't taste like *beans*? There is no strange taste in this Cake, just that **great taste** of *chocolate*, yum.

(For the cake in the photo I doubled the recipe and baked them in round cake pans, stacked them and made a very large, and very happy birthday cake.)

Ingredients

Dry
1 cup UNflour (see page 12)
¼ cup cornstarch
1 teaspoon xanthan gum
1 cup sugar
½ teaspoon salt
1 teaspoon baking powder
½ teaspoon baking soda
¾ cup cocoa

Wet
1 ½ cup milk (or milk substitute)
1 egg
¼ cup canola or vegetable oil
1 teaspoon vanilla

Directions

1. Preheat oven to 350 degrees.
2. Combine all dry ingredients in mixing bowl.
3. While mixing pour in milk, eggs, oil, and vanilla.
4. Beat on high 2 minutes.
5. Pour into two greased 8- or 9-inch round pans or one 9x13-inch baking dish. (Or for 15-18 cupcakes, line a muffin tin with cupcake papers, filling about ½ full.)
6. Bake for about 40-45 minutes for cake, and 30 minutes for cupcakes, or until toothpick tests clean in center.
7. Cool and frost.

Easy Cream Cheese Frosting

Combine the following ingredients in mixing bowl:

3 cups powdered sugar
4 tablespoons butter (slightly softened)
4 oz cream cheese
¼ cup (more or less) milk
½ tsp salt
2 teaspoons vanilla
Food coloring if desired

Mix well and spread on cake or use to decorate.

White Cake

This **White Cake** is very *versatile*.
Use it in ***family favorite recipes*** like **pineapple-upside-down Cake**. Or **create** something new. It even works great in **cookie** recipes that call for a **White or Yellow Cake** mix.

Ingredients

Dry

1 ½ cup UNflour (see page 12)
½ cup cornstarch
1 teaspoon xanthan gum
1 cup sugar
½ teaspoon salt
1 teaspoon baking powder
½ teaspoon baking soda
2 teaspoons Amaretto coffee
   creamer *(optional, but excellent!)*

Wet

1 ½ cups milk (or milk substitute)
1 egg
¼ cup canola or vegetable oil
1 teaspoon vanilla
½ teaspoon butter flavor extract

Directions

1. Preheat oven to 350 degrees.
2. Combine all dry ingredients in mixing bowl.
3. While mixing pour in milk, eggs, oil and flavorings.
4. Beat on high 2 minutes.
5. Pour into two greased 8- or 9-inch round pans or one 9x13-inch baking dish. (Or for 15-18 cupcakes, line a muffin tin with cupcake papers, filling about ½ full.)
6. Bake for about 40-45 minutes for cake, and 30 minutes for cupcakes, or until toothpick tests clean in center.
7. Cool and frost.

Doughnuts

How many times has **your child's class** had a Doughnut party? It *breaks my heart*, thinking of my child eating a *sucker* while **everyone else** is having Doughnuts! So, I went to work, and here is a Doughnut **your kids will love!**

Ingredients

Dry
⅔ cup UNflour (see page 12)
½ cup cornstarch
½ cup tapioca flour
1 teaspoon xanthan gum
⅓ cup sugar
½ teaspoon salt
1 tablespoon baking powder

Wet
1 teaspoon vanilla
½ cup milk (or milk substitute)
1 egg
2 tablespoons canola or
    vegetable oil

For steps 7-10
2-3 cups canola or vegetable oil
½ cup powdered sugar for topping

Directions

1. Combine all dry ingredients (except powdered sugar) in heavy mixer.

2. While mixing on low, add wet ingredients.

3. Mix well to remove lumps. Dough will be thick enough to handle, but sticky.

4. Dust countertop with cornstarch. Scrape dough onto dusted countertop, then sprinkle a dusting of cornstarch on top of dough and pat out dough to about ¼ inch thick.

5. Using a round cookie cutter (or an empty and clean tuna fish can), cut out doughnuts.

6. Cut a center hole for each doughnut using a small round object (I have been known to use a plastic water bottle lid).

7. Heat the oil for frying in a frying pan to 360 degrees, or use a deep fryer.

8. Place each doughnut in the hot oil until light brown, turn over and brown other side.

9. Remove to paper towel to drain excess oil.

10. While doughnuts are still warm, rub one side in powdered sugar, then set aside to finish cooling. Repeat this for each doughnut and doughnut hole.

    Makes about 10 doughnuts *(and 10 doughnut holes!)*

These doughnuts are best fresh, but will keep for a day or two in an airtight container.

IrresistiblyGlutenFree: Simple Family Favorite R

Cinnamon Rolls

The **nuts** in this recipe **are optional**, and **my kids** prefer their *gluten-free* Cinnamon Rolls **without**. The topping gives them a **candy coating** that is just as *delicious* as it is *sticky*, so be prepared to **lick your fingers!**

Ingredients

Dry

1 ¾ cups UNflour (see page 12)
1 teaspoon xanthan gum
¼ cup instant dry milk
    (or almond meal)
½ cup sugar
½ teaspoon salt
1 teaspoon baking powder
1 tablespoon instant dry yeast

Wet

1 cup warm water
2 tablespoons butter slightly
    softened or shortening
1 egg

Filling

¾ cup sugar
1 tablespoon ground cinnamon
½ cup chopped pecans

Topping

2 tablespoons butter
¼ cup brown sugar
¼ cup corn syrup

Directions

1. Combine filling ingredients, set aside.
2. Combine dry ingredients in mixer.
3. Add warm water and shortening while mixing on low. Add egg and beat on high for about 2 minutes.
4. In well-greased muffin tin, put 1 rounded tablespoon batter in each muffin cup.
5. Top with 1 teaspoon filling mixture.
6. Put another tablespoon of batter in each cup, and smooth top with wet fingers to cover the filling underneath.
7. Top with another ½ teaspoon filling. Set rolls aside to rise for 20 mintures or until double in size.
8. Mix topping ingredients in a small saucepan and melt together on low heat.
9. Using a large spoon, top each roll with a spoonful of topping.
10. Bake in preheated oven at 350 degrees for 30 minutes.
11. Using a fork in each hand, remove rolls from tins while hot (or they will stick to pan!). Put each roll upside down on a plate to cool.

Makes 12 rolls.

Graham Crackers

Okay, so **my husband** thought I was **crazy** when I handed him a homemade, *gluten-free* Graham Cracker, but **my kids** were elated! **"We can have** *S'mores!***"** And don't let them intimidate you, they are a lot like making Sugar Cookies.

Ingredients

Dry

2 cups UNflour (see page 12)
1 teaspoon xanthan gum
1 ½ cups brown sugar
1 teaspoon salt
1 tablespoon baking powder
¾ teaspoon cinnamon

Wet

½ cup (1 cube) butter, slightly softened
1 teaspoon vanilla
⅓ cup water

These graham crackers can be crushed and used to make a graham-cracker pie crust by mixing crushed crackers with a little melted butter and pressing firmly into a pie pan.

Directions

1. Put dry ingredients in the bowl of a heavy mixer.

2. With mixer on low add wet ingredients to dry. After mixing for about 2 minutes, dough should start to form a ball. (If it looks a little too wet to form a ball it could just be that the butter was too soft; it may firm up in the refrigerator. If it is too dry, add a little more water.)

3. Remove from mixer. Dough should resemble a large ball of firm play dough.

4. Preheat oven to 320 degrees. Grease cookie sheet, set aside.

5. Divide dough in half, and roll out to ¼ inch thick on countertop dusted with cornstarch.

6. You can cut the dough into rectangles, or use a cookie cutter of your choice. Cut out dough and place on cookie sheet.

7. Bake for 12-15 minutes. They will feel soft, but firm up as they cool.

8. To make them look like a real graham cracker use a fork to poke holes and a pizza cutter to trim the edges while cookies are cooling.

9. Cool on cookie sheet for 5-8 minutes. (The longer they cool on the sheet the crispier they will be.)
Makes about 2 dozen.

About the author...

Christina Davis had always been told by medical professionals that her wheat intolerance was "all in her head." As it turns out, they were wrong; it was all in her digestive system.

Christina always knew she had issues with bread and pasta, but didn't learn she was celiac until she was 21. She is now married with six children, three of which are also celiac.

Christina has learned that you don't have to give up your favorite foods to eat gluten free. She embarked on a quest to create gluten-free foods that taste good, are simple to make, and most importantly, are foods her kids will eat. She has now been cooking gluten free for 15 years and helping others along the way to make the transition. This cookbook has evolved from the recipes she most frequently uses and shares with others who are looking for support.

About the photographer...

Shawn Robins is a portrait, landscape, and food photographer, located in the Pacific Northwest. His photography has been featured in *Ancestry* Magazine as well as local publications and web sites in Washington State. His passion for photography surrounds his life especially when his family and food are involved. You can see more of Shawn's work at www.shawnrobins.com.